# Celebrities' Lessons in Estate Planning™

## AN EASY-TO-READ GUIDE TO ESTATE PLANNING

Jeanne M. Kerkstra, Esq., CPA

© 2016–2024 by Jeanne M. Kerkstra

All rights reserved. Except as permitted under the U.S. Copyright Act of 1976, no part of this publication may be reproduced, distributed, or transmitted in any form or by any means, or stored in a database or retrieval system, without the prior written permission of the publisher.

The names and logos of *Celebrities' Lessons in Estate Planning* are trademarks of Jeanne M. Kerkstra.

**Disclaimer:** The following are the opinions of this author. They are based to the best of my knowledge on information gleaned from business and entertainment news.

To my sons for their encouragement
and my clients for their inspiration

# GIFTS TO LOVED ONES, NOT UNCLE SAM

**ACT NOW** before the December 31, 2025 **critical deadline** for minimizing your federal estate and gift tax exposure. In 2024, this exemption is a healthy $13,610,000 per individual or $27,220,000 per married couple. This drastically plummets to its pre-2018 levels of $5,000,000 (adjusted for inflation estimated between $6,000,000 – $7,000,000 per individual or $12,000,000 – $14,000,000 per married couple).

There are many options to consider to be tailored to your unique needs including SLATs, QPRTs, GRATs, DAPTs, CRTs, and more. If you do not want to pay a large chunk of your legacy to the federal government but want to pass it on to your loved ones, immediately check out the advanced estate planning options on page 47. These options take time to consider and to set up.

Call me for an appointment before it is too late.

**Jeanne M. Kerkstra, Esq., CPA**
**312.285.9147**

# Prologue

Celebrities are just like us. Oh, yes, they are. They just do everything on a larger scale. Mistakes. Transgressions. Fuck up's. All in the public eye with paparazzi waiting (hoping) for them to screw up.

And, as they say, nothing in life is for certain except death & taxes. People ask me when they hear about celebrities not doing their estate plan: why is that? Is there a law somehow prohibiting it? No. They are just like us: they procrastinate, and/or they have drama playing out in their lives preventing them. Why should people do estate planning? For some of us to save taxes but for all of us for privacy. The good news (sarcastic tone) is if you don't have an estate plan, the State where you reside upon your death will have laws designating who gets what (for example, the musician Prince). The bad news is that it is played out all before the public (three-ring circus).

My goal as an attorney/Certified Public Accountant is not to bore you but rather educate you on how to avoid probate in order to keep your estate confidential and to legitimately keep estate taxes to a minimum. Remember, if you don't like tax loopholes, champion to change them. Since they are legal and they can help you, use them.

# What is Probate?

Many famous celebrities' estates have to be probated when they pass. Recent examples are the musicians Prince and Michael Jackson but for vastly different reasons. Although probate laws in different States are similar, there may be differences. That is why for the most part we are talking about what happens if you pass away in Illinois.

If your estate has to be probated, what does that mean? It is a legal proceeding that is public. It's costly. It's time-consuming and could lead to possibly more litigation if something is contested. Now I have to point out that not everyone is probate-adverse like me. I once did a seminar together with a good colleague who has a successful law practice as a probate litigator. He started his portion asking emphatically, "What the Hell is wrong with probate?" To some, nothing. People will tell you that you can pay legal fees now to set up an estate plan and fund it (move assets into it) or later once you pass away when it has to be probated. [I understand that attorneys are less popular than used car salesmen, but it is ultimately up to you, much like the lesser of two evils.]

In Illinois, if you pass away with any real estate or greater than $100,000 in personal property solely in your name, your estate must be probated (it goes before a court). Back up a moment. You might ask: what is personal property? Good question. Personal property is anything other than real estate. It includes household furniture (but not the house, which is real estate), cars, jewelry, stamps and coin collections, and boats. In other words, if it is not real estate, it is personal property.

Someone who had attended my seminar came up to me and told me that he had large farmland holdings in downstate Illinois. It was a small community where everyone knew everybody's business, so he didn't mind that he just had a Will. It would be probated, and everyone would know who got what. I asked him, "Wouldn't it be great if you could pull a fast one on them? Get a 'gotcha!' from beyond the grave by moving while you are alive everything into a Revocable Trust which becomes irrevocable upon your passing." A Revocable Trust (aka Living Trust) is a confidential document and doesn't get publicly recorded. When you have a Revocable Trust, you also have a pour-over Will, which contains minimal information and is recorded upon your death in the county in which you resided. His neighbors could get a copy of the recorded Will only to find out that it simply said he had a Trust. Only beneficiaries under a Trust are privy to any information. Oh, what a "gotcha!" moment. Nevertheless, everyone has to feel comfortable with whatever they put in place, and he wanted a Will. So, upon his passing, all of his assets would need to be probated.

Ok, so say you have in your name alone upon your passing any real estate or personal property worth more than $100,000. Then what? Well, if you die without a Will or nobody can find your estate plan, then you have died intestate, which means your State's law dictates who gets what. We'll talk more about that in a moment. If you die with a Will, congratulations, you are a testator, and your Will dictates who gets what. Remember these court proceedings are almost always open to the public. Your estate representative goes before a judge in probate court, and it is determined who are heirs and legatees (who has rights to your assets per State law). Your assets (anything you own) are inventoried, and creditors have six months to file claims against your estate. After all your debts have been paid and the court proceedings are wrapped up, the final step is to distribute your assets.

There are strange creatures called Will Vultures. They are unscrupulous individuals who copy Wills, which are public documents, and see if they can file a Will contest, which may be a frivolous claim against your estate. Will Vultures are despicable creatures.

# Passing Away Intestate (Without a Will)

What happens if you die without a Will and no other estate plan? You have died intestate. Where your assets go depends on whether you were married and had children. If you were married and had children, then ½ of your estate goes to your spouse and the other ½ goes to your children per stirpes. It simply means that if one of your children passes before you, that child's share goes to his/her children. In other words, it goes down the bloodline. If you had a spouse but no children, then your entire estate goes to your spouse. If you did not have a spouse but had children, it all goes to your children. If you did not have a spouse or children, it goes equally to your parents and siblings. See the nifty chart below that summarizes all of this.

| INTESTACY MATRIX | Descendants | No Descendants |
|---|---|---|
| **Surviving Spouse** | 1/2 to Surviving Spouse and 1/2 to Descendants (per stirpes) | All to Surviving Spouse |
| **No Surviving Spouse** | All to Descendants (per stirpes) | Equally to Parents and Siblings |

Hip-hop artist, Earl Simmons, better known as DMX and Dark Man X, sold over 74 million records worldwide. He passed away from a heart attack, possibly after a drug overdose. He did not have a Will and was not married at the time of his death. His estate will go to his children, and he is believed to have had 15 children with 9 women. The starting

DMX

point will be determining his legitimate heirs. Remember, even if his estate has massive debt like Michael Jackson's, his heirs will own all the rights to his music from his date of death (regardless of how long it may take to settle this matter). Unlike most people, recording artists make money after their deaths, which can even eclipse their lifetime earnings, especially because so many die so young. Whoever owns these rights reaps the rewards, and here it will be DMX's heirs.

A sad thing about life is how unexpected it can be. People have so much passion and energy. They make a loving and lasting impact on those around them. Chadwick Boseman was one such individual – a phenomenal actor who leaves a wealth of astounding movies (42, Marshall, Get on Up, Black Panther) yet whose life was cut far too short at 43 from colon cancer. Mr.

*Chadwick Boseman*

Boseman left an intestate estate valued at around $1 million. Intestate means leaving no Will. He had married his longtime girlfriend a few months before his passing. They had no children. According to state law, it would all pass to her. But, as discussed later, most people wish to have their assets pass privately, outside of probate via confidential Trusts and transfers automatically upon death known as POD's and TOD's. Presumably, that is how much of Mr. Boseman's assets passed – discreetly and outside the public's prying eyes.

# CELEBRITIES' LESSONS IN ESTATE PLANNING

Herman Cain was known for many things – CEO of the National Restaurant Association and 2012 Republican Presidential Candidate, to name just a couple. When he passed away unexpectedly in late 2020, it was discovered that he had no Will. A probate estate was opened to name an Administrator to handle the distribution of estate assets of about

*Herman Cain*

$585,000 to the appropriate beneficiaries after proper estate claims are paid. That's when things got interesting over a seemingly low amount. Lisa Reichert, Mr. Cain's assistant for over nine years, claimed she was owed about $52,500 as a severance package in line with what had been paid to former assistants. Probate matters are overwhelmingly open to public scrutiny, which is why many of my clients seek to avoid having their estates probated. Ms. Reichart claimed Mr. Cain had gold bars and coins and cash in a safe deposit box which were not disclosed on Mrs. Cain's sworn Petition. The Petition listed real estate in Henry County, Georgia worth about $103,900 and cash/bank accounts/CD's of about $25,000 and stocks/bonds/brokerage accounts of about $457,000. Further, Ms. Reichart claimed to know of additional assets not listed on the Petition. Again, probate is public, and we will all see how this plays out, which is why most of my clients strive for privacy.

Now some of you may have heard about the musician Prince, who was a phenomenal musician, producer and actor. His parents had passed away, and he had a full sister and five half brothers and sisters. When Prince passed away in April 2016, his full sister went before the Minnesota probate court and declared that Prince had no Will. Illinois and Minnesota have similar probate laws. Now because he had no Will, his estate would pass according to the chart above. When Prince died, his estate was immediately valued by some sources at $100 million. That is just a figure bantered about. Besides all his published songs, Prince allegedly had a vault of unpublished songs. All of Prince's assets would have to be appraised at fair market value. Any estate worth more than $5.45 million in 2016 had to file a federal estate tax return (Form 706). Anything over $5.45 million was taxed by the IRS at 40%. In 2016, Minnesota also required the filing of a State estate tax return for estates over $1.8 million. So Prince's estate would also be filing this return and paying Minnesota estate tax. If Prince did not have any children, then his full sister and half brothers and sisters would all equally share in his estate.

Although Prince's body was cremated, they still had his DNA. At least one person came forward and declared that he was Prince's son, and he was incarcerated at the time. However, if he could prove through the blood tests that he was Prince's son, he would take all. In the end, the DNA test proved he was not his son, so Prince's siblings would inherit everything.

*Prince*

As with other large estates like Michael Jackson, the IRS has disputed the purported valuation of his estate. His estate representatives claimed about $80 million, while the IRS claims about $160 million. That translates into about $65 million in taxes. While this battle is fought in tax court, his heirs wait for an outcome. Remember this has been going on since Prince's death in 2016.

In January 2022, Comerica Bank, the administrator of the estate agreed with the IRS valuation of the estate of $156.4 million. Three of Prince's heirs, two of them deceased, had sold their interests to the publishing company, Primary Wave. Three of Prince's siblings retained their interests. The IRS will receive a significant tax payment—about $65 million—and interest owing for the past six years. But the heirs and Primary Wave will receive the income from anything after Prince's 2016 death, which includes lucrative streaming and sales royalties, and advertising such as in movies and TV.

Anthony Chia-Hua Hsieh founded Zappos, an online shoe and clothing company. In 2020, just after retiring, he died at age 47 in a strange house fire. He had no wife or children and it turned out no Will. So his entire estate valued at about $840 million will pass though probate court for all to see.

*Anthony Chia-Hua Hsieh*

Twice widowed Tom Benson, owner of the New Orleans NFL Saints and NBA Pelicans was married to his third wife, Gayle Benson, when he died in 2018. They had been married since 2004. There was a protracted fight while he was alive with his daughter—Renee Benson—and his grandchildren—Rita & Ryan LeBlanc—from a previous marriage and known as

*Tom Benson*

the 3Rs. In 2015 he fired the 3Rs alleging they were always disrespectful to Gayle. The 3Rs took him to court alleging he was incompetent. The judge ruled in Tom's favor finding that, like the average person his age (close to 90), he had some cognitive issues but was competent to make succession planning decisions. This decision was upheld in the higher courts. Immediately after the ruling, Tom drafted a new Will naming Gayle, his spouse, as the sole owner of the NFL Saints and NBA Pelicans. Tom died March 15, 2018. It should be noted the 3Rs sued in two separate cases and settled, receiving valuable assets including where Tom had clawed back non-controlling stock in the Saints and Pelicans as well as receiving bank branches, car dealerships and a hunting ranch.

So how does that apply to the average family dynamics? Blended families are rather common nowadays. No matter what their age, if a loved one is demonstrating that they may be materially impaired, it is warranted to raise the issue and have them assessed for their own well-being. If competent, there now is a baseline. If incompetent, Powers of Attorney

(POAs) come into play and possibly guardianship proceedings. All of this is for the loved one's own protection – physically and financially.

It is important to note that, at times, competency is a highly fluid situation. Someone may be competent at certain times of the day but not others. Further, a person may be competent to make a Will but be incompetent for business succession planning. To be competent, a main point is that a person must know the natural objects of their bounty (e.g., spouse and kids), but it is probably the hardest thing for us to admit we are losing it and accept help.

# Passing Away Testate (With a Will)

Gina Lollobrigida passed away in Italy on January 16, 2023 at the age of 95, having a prolific life as an actress, sculptor, mother, and more. In the '80s, she retired from acting, so Gina had many life chapters. In her final years, she was embroiled in troubling litigation. One lawsuit was against Javier Rigau y Rafols, a former boyfriend of 20 years, who was 34 years her junior, and in which she alleged their marriage was a fraud. It sounded quite like a Hollywood script, with Gina alleging Javier had manipulated her into signing a consent to marry him and the wedding allegedly happening with a stand-in for Gina.

*Gina Lollobrigida*

A mere four years later, in 2021, Gina's son, Mike Skofic, Jr., who was 62 years old at the time, took her to court, claiming she was incompetent. Her manager, Andrea Piazzolla, then 31, allegedly was selling some of her real estate and pricey sports cars and giving the proceeds to his parents. Gina hired a mafia-busting attorney to go up against her son. It was my understanding that she retained control of her day-to-day expenses but lost control of her asset management.

Her Will split her assets between her son and her manager. Note her manager had started with Gina as her driver when he was 24 and continually got greater responsibility. It was reported that he eventually moved in with Gina along with his boyfriend and having named their baby girl after Gina.

Now what? A Will challenge? Is there a law against what the manager did? I don't know about Italian law, but in Illinois we have a law that cautions against such behavior. Effective January 1, 2015, Illinois enacted Section 4a-10 of the Probate Act (entitled, "Presumptively Void Transfers") which states, "In any civil action in which a transfer instrument is being challenged, there is a rebuttable presumption, except as provided in Section 4a-15, that the transfer instrument is void if the transferee is a caregiver and the fair market value of the transferred property exceeds $20,000." For those who are caregivers but not family members, this gift may be capped or voidable entirely. The definition of "Caregiver" is broad and means a person who voluntarily, or in exchange for compensation, has assumed responsibility for all or a portion of the care of another person who needs assistance with activities of daily living. "Caregiver" includes a caregiver's spouse, cohabitant, child, or employee. "Caregiver" does not include a family member of the person receiving assistance. In any lawsuit filed to challenge this gift, the Caregiver has the burden to prove the validity of the transfer by clear and convincing evidence. Under section, 4a-15, the rebuttable presumption established by Section 4a-10 can be overcome if you can prove to the court that the transfer was not the product of fraud, duress, or undue influence. The law states that if you fail to prove these things, you shall bear the costs of the proceedings, including, without limitation, reasonable attorney's fees. This Illinois law is amazing! Employees and cohabitants are now under great scrutiny in Illinois which is trying to prevent elder abuse – which sadly cannot only be physical but financial.

The Queen of Soul passed in 2018. Following her death, Wills were discovered in a locked cabinet as well as in-between sofa cushions.

The question was which, if either, was her binding Will. One had a condition: get a degree or get nothing. Aretha had 4 sons, one who is disabled and financially provided for. In 2023, the court finally made a decision that the valid Will was the one in-between the sofa cushions and without the condition. This legal finding took years, cost money and caused many people stress, all of which was avoidable with some planning and decision-making. By making your wishes known, it has to be shown respect and that is spelt: R…E…S…P…E…C…T.

*Aretha Franklin*

Remember, with any estate plan you should update it when there is any birth, death, marriage or divorce. The importance of staying updated can be understood by examining Heath Ledger's death. Heath Ledger came from Australia to the U.S. to make it big in Hollywood. Among many other movies, he starred in Brokeback Mountain and got an Oscar posthumously for his role as the Joker in the Dark Knight. He was single when he drafted a Will stating that all his assets would pass equally to his parents and siblings. In 2004, he and actress Michelle Williams started dating. In 2005, they had a baby, Matilda. In 2007, they broke up. In January, 2008, he passed away from an alleged accidental overdose. The only estate plan that he had was his Will which left everything equally to his parents and siblings. He had gone from a "starving artist" to a renowned actor worth over $20 million. All of that was to be split equally between his parents and siblings, meaning his infant daughter was to receive nothing. However, Heath's parents and siblings generously agreed that his daughter should have the value of his estate attributed to the U.S. income or about $16.5 million. The lesson here is you want to make sure your estate passes how you want it to, so remember to review your

*Heath Ledger*

estate plan whenever there is a birth, death, marriage or divorce.

Larry King, world-renowned interviewer, passed away in 2021. He left a very brief (less than 50 words) Will handwritten in October, 2019, while he was in the middle of divorce proceedings. Accomplishing all you want is daunting in a 50-word Will. Key terms were omitted. Executors – those in charge – weren't named. His 2019 Will left everything equally to his 5 children, but tragically 2 of them predeceased him in 2020. His Will does not specify if his estate was to pass to his children per stirpes (that means down the bloodline of a deceased child) or per capita (that means with the balance equally to the surviving siblings). All of this uncertainty will play out in a very public setting – probate court. Note that only assets in Larry's name alone will pass through his Will. Presumably, most of his assets would be in the name of a Trust and pass via this confidential document. Lastly, because this was not his first marriage – 8th in fact – odds are that the couple had a pre-marital agreement in place before they were married, which would keep each person's separate property separate.

*Larry King*

If you have a Revocable Trust (aka Living Trust) but do not fund it during your life, then your estate will have to go through probate for the assets to get to your Trust. The downside with this is that your assets are public knowledge. The upside is that your beneficiaries who receive those assets remain confidential. An example is Tom Clancy, the prolific author, whose books were turned into blockbuster movies. Many of them starred Harrison Ford, such ones as The Hunt for Red October and Patriot Games. Amazingly his books were also turned into wildly successful video

*Tom Clancy*

game series including Ghost Recon, Splinter Cell, and Rainbow Six. His estate was worth an alleged $200 million. He had a Revocable Trust, but it was not funded before his death. A revocable trust is considered not funded when assets are not retitled into the name of the Trust or the beneficiary designations are not changed to the Trust. Remember that any real estate or greater than $100,000 in personal property in your name alone upon your death has to be probated.

The court battle would center on who would pay the estate tax. At his death, he was married to his 2nd wife, who was from a well off Coca-Cola distributorship and about 30 years his junior. So she came to the marriage with money. His 1st wife and his children (all from his 1st marriage) were taken care of during his divorce. Within a year before his death, Tom's estate plan was changed to include that any estate tax would not be paid by his 2nd wife. The attorney who drafted this was also the Executor of Tom's estate. The Executor is in charge of any assets that flow through the Will. It is reasonable to presume that any changes made within a year before death are more closely scrutinized for competency, undue influence, or duress. Tom had major assets passing through probate including his $65 million Baltimore Orioles ownership, but many assets avoided probate including an $11 million 17,000 sq. ft. Ritz-Carlton condo because this was held as joint tenants with his 2nd wife. Joint tenants mean the last one standing gets it all. Tom and his 2nd wife owned the condo as joint tenants so, by operation of law, his 2nd wife automatically owned it by herself upon Tom's passing. Presumably, his legal team advised him to move those considerable assets in his name alone into his Revocable Trust. Why didn't Tom avoid probate? Who knows?

A lot of times the main problem with going through probate is that it is played out in public and becomes a three-ring circus. Dirty laundry is aired, and family fights are exposed. Despite this, sometimes a

*David Bowie*

probate proceeding can be very cut and dry and devoid of drama. This can happen even with large estates. Take for example the probate of the Will of David Robert Jones, whose estate was allegedly valued at $100 million. You may not recognize David Robert Jones because he never legally took his stage name, David Bowie.

To me, David Bowie was an astonishing artist – incredibly impacting fashion, music, movies and so much more. He had his son when he was 24 years old and allegedly said that his son watched him mature. He was an incredible businessman who marketed Bowie Bonds around 1997 whereby he sold 10 years of royalties from his 1st 25 albums and received about $55 million for them. After the royalty period expired, all rights reverted back to him. Genius! Also, with the rise of the internet, life had become so public for all of us. It seemed like anything was on the web. In 2004, when he was performing in Europe, he seemed to slump on one side. He thought he had pinched a nerve and kept going. It turned out he had a heart attack. Soon David Bowie would tour no more. However, he remained artistic, and in the final years of his life, he had a burst of creativity. I won't forget how his final album, Blackstar, was released on a Friday, and his passing was announced that following Monday morning. I couldn't believe what my favorite radio station was saying about one of my all-time favorite performers. He will be sorely missed, but his memory will always live on. Under his Will, his wife, Iman, received 50%. His son received 25%, and David's teenage daughter, because of her age, received the remaining 25% in trust.

Let's review. If you do not have a Will or no one can find your estate plan when you pass, then you have died intestate (without a Will), and your estate must be probated. The State in which you pass away has an estate plan for you built into its probate laws. If you only have a Will, your estate must be probated. If you have a Revocable Trust (aka Living Trust) but do not transfer any assets into it or designate any beneficiaries to it during your life, your estate will be probated to get these assets into your Revocable Trust. Examples of this include Tom Clancy, who was mentioned above, and the recording artist Michael Jackson.

Michael Jackson also had a Revocable Trust which he did not fund while he was alive. Upon his death, there was a huge media circus with the probate proceedings. First of all, remember that a Will almost always is a public document that anyone can get a copy of. Secondly, Wills and Revocable Trusts almost always contain "no contest" clauses, which mean if you argue that you should get more, you get nothing. The reason for this is straightforward: it is the deceased's right (for the most part) to pass his/her estate as they want. Note that you cannot disinherit your spouse, but you can disinherit your children. We will discuss this more later.

*Michael Jackson*

The main problem in Michael's estate was that he did not fund his Revocable Trust before death so that it played out for all to see in probate court. Another problem was that his mother apparently wasn't named as either Executor under his Will or even more importantly as Trustee under his Trust. His mother had to tread carefully when she brought an action to argue about the appointment of the Executors. She had to make sure she wasn't seen as contesting his Will. Otherwise, she would have legally been deemed to have passed before Michael, and her share would have gone to his children.

In today's world with easy access to the internet, everything seems to be exposed and posted on it – even Michael Jackson's confidential Family Trust. We should never give up the fight for privacy because it is tremendously important to keep. The more we lose our privacy, the more we lose a part of ourselves.

To some it may be interesting to note that upon Michael's passing his representatives valued his estate at about $10,000. They argued that his estate couldn't be worth more due to the devastating impact of the child molestation charges. However, the IRS paid particular attention to this case. Remember, anything over the federal estate tax exemption is taxable. Michael died in 2009 when the federal estate tax exemption was $3,500,000, and the top federal estate tax rate was 45%. That means his net taxable estate over $3,500,000 was taxed at 45%. Since his death, his estate has allegedly sold over $600,000,000 in products. For estate tax valuation, you look at the value of his estate at his death or 9 months later if the value decreased. The value certainly did not decrease. But what was it on his date of death? He seemed to have an insatiable appetite for spending. And, he had considerable debts. So what was the real value of his estate?

On May 3, 2021, the 271-page opinion of the Tax Court come down. The crux of its decision is that assets are valued at the date of death, and do not include any future marketing or management opportunities. Only the valuation of three assets were litigated. Michael Jackson's image and likeness was valued on the federal estate tax return at $2,105. The IRS exam estimated its value at $434,000,000. Definitely a worthwhile reason to litigate. The court determined its value at about $4,000,000. To understand the valuation, you have to remember all that was happening right before his unexpected demise, and it wasn't pretty.

The second asset was his ownership in Sony. The estate tax return valued it at $0, while the IRS exam claimed it was worth about $470,000,000. This was a heavily-leveraged asset because Michael Jackson was in such debt. Accordingly, the court valued it at $0.

The final asset litigated was his ownership in MIJAC, which owns copyrights in musicians including his own. The estate tax return valued it at about $2,200,000, while the IRS claimed it worth about $58,500,000. The court valued it at about $107,314,000.

Remember for estate tax purposes, it is what it is worth at death, not what happens to the asset after death. The attorneys for the estate scored a big win (saving beneficiaries a lot of money) for 2 of the 3 assets. The question is whether the parties will appeal and draw out the litigation even longer.

# Avoiding Probate – Alternatives with Downsides

So what isn't included in your probate estate? Well, assets that are already funded (to be discussed more later) in your Revocable Trust; assets in joint tenancy; and when beneficiaries are already designated such as on life insurance and retirement plans.

Let's talk about alternatives to probate. One is known as the poor-man's Will where you add a parent, sibling or friend as joint tenant to your assets and direct them as to how to divide it up upon your passing. There are 2 problems with this. First, when you add someone to the title of your asset, you open this asset up to the claims of their creditors. Secondly, once you are gone, you are gone. You will never know for sure if they followed your directions.

I like to refer to the following as the alphabet soup of probate alternatives: TBE, POD, TOD, and TODI.

If you are married and want creditor protection (a beautiful thing when needed), depending on the State in which you live in, you can hold certain assets as Tenants by the Entirety (aka TBE). TBE is rooted in the centuries' old belief in the sanctity of marriage. If creditors have a claim against one spouse but not the other, they cannot attach (get their hands on) the assets. In Illinois, we are skimpy with TBE possibilities. We have one: you can hold your personal residence as TBE, which is a good thing because people want to keep their homes. In other States like Delaware and Florida, you can hold anything as TBE (now that's a really beautiful thing). TBE is a very special form of joint tenancy that only married couples can do. As with joint tenancy, TBE means the last one standing gets it all by operation of law, and it is not included in the first deceased's estate.

Pay on Death (POD) means just that. You designate while you are alive who will be paid on death. This is typical for bank accounts, certificates of deposits, and savings bonds.

Transfer on Death (TOD) means just that. You designate while you are alive who will be paid upon your death. This is typical for investment accounts.

Transfer on Death Instruments (TODI) are an unusual type of deed for real estate. Typically a deed transfers ownership now. Although a TODI is signed now, it only transfers ownership upon your death. Also, under a TODI, your beneficiaries have an affirmative obligation to come forward after your death within 2 years and affirm that they want the transfer.

If you die with no real estate and less than $100,000 of personal property in your name alone, your representative gets something like a "Get out of Jail Free card". It is called a Small Estate Affidavit. This allows the assets (less than $100,000 worth of personal property) to pass to the beneficiaries without having to go through probate (another beautiful thing).

You might ask: why fund a Revocable Trust before your death? Good question. There are many good reasons. It ensures that assets go when and where you want. It gives special creditor protection to trust beneficiaries (other than the Grantor who establishes the Trust) if the

# CELEBRITIES' LESSONS IN ESTATE PLANNING | 25

assets remain in Trust upon the Grantor's passing. It avoids probate. It is fully revocable, which means you can cancel it at any time until you are incompetent or pass away. While you are alive, revocable trusts have no tax effect. It plans for disability; the successor trustee takes over your financial affairs upon your incompetency or death. You will want to tie in the successor trustees named in your Revocable Trust with your agents named in your durable Power of Attorney for Property, which we will discuss later.

Why engage in estate planning? To remain in control upon your incompetency or passing. Let's talk about several examples.

First, there is Bing Crosby, the legendary crooner and actor. Now I know I am dating myself. Was Bing Crosby an example of tough love or Scrooge? You decide. He didn't want his children to grow up as children of a celebrity. He wanted them to work for a living so he set up a trust where none of his children could receive anything until he/she were 65 years old, and some of them didn't make it that long.

*Bing Crosby*

Second is Whitney Houston, a phenomenal singer and actress who allegedly had many demons. When she passed away, Whitney was allegedly worth $30 million. Her assets were in her Trust at the time of her death. We only know about distributions that were made public. For example, it became known that her daughter, Bobbi Kristina Brown, would get a $2 million distribution at the age of 21. She allegedly also had demons similar to her mother. It is rumored that the money came out of the trust when Bobbi turned 21 but after that she suffered a terrible accident which left

*Whitney Houston*

her on life-support and she died shortly thereafter. You might ask: what happened to the rest of the money in Whitney's Trust? We don't know. Why? Because a Trust is a private document. It is confidential. Unless someone leaks the document, we will never know. We are not entitled to know. The only ones who are entitled to know are the beneficiaries. And, that is how it should be.

Third is Aaron Spelling, who seemed to basically create T&A before the web existed. He created Charlie's Angels, Beverly Hills 90210, T.J. Hooker, The Love Boat and so much more. When he passed, he was worth a reported $500 million. During his life, his wife, Candy, thought that their daughter, Tori, might have a spending problem. Can someone have a spending problem when their father is worth $500 million? Can you really burn through that much money? One thing's for sure, I'll never know. Regardless Aaron took steps to create a Trust and put his wife, Candy, in charge. Remember, you cannot disinherit your spouse, but you can disinherit your children.

*Aaron Spelling*

In over 20 years of practicing law, some of my clients have disinherited their children in a variety of ways. First, some simply name that child and say they are leaving them nothing. Others name the child and leave them $100, $1,000 or $25,000. This statement coupled with a "no contest" clause prevents them from getting anything more under their parents' estate plan. So, Aaron apparently wanted to disinherit his children, Tori and Randy. If you were worth $500 million, how would you do it? Well, he left each of them $800,000. Tori has said before that she was born with a silver spoon in her mouth and then had to live with plastic. Fun fact: How many rooms were in the Spelling Manor? Hint: 3 rooms were simply for gift wrapping. My younger son asked: what kinds of gifts? I don't know. Just gift wrapping. Guess? Answer: 123.

Lesson: You can disinherit your children but not your spouse. Better be nice to your parents.

Lisa Marie Presley passed away on January 12, 2023, at the age of 54. She was Elvis Presley's only child and sole heir to his estate. In recent years Lisa Marie was in the news for litigation with her manager, who she claimed left her broke and with him countersuing for unpaid bills and claiming Lisa Marie had extravagant spending habits. The litigation was still ongoing at the time of her death.

Lisa Marie Presley

Lisa Marie's mother, Priscilla Presley, is contesting her daughter's alleged amendment to her estate plan whereby Lisa Marie removed her mother and her manager as co-Trustees and replaced them with her two oldest children – daughter, Riley Keough, and son, Benjamin Keough. Benjamin committed suicide in July, 2020, devastating Lisa Marie and her family. If Lisa Marie's estate plan is deemed valid by the courts, Riley would be the sole Trustee of Lisa Marie's estate.

Although at the time of her death, Lisa Marie's estate may not have had significant liquid assets, it is reported to hold a 15% ownership in Elvis Presley Enterprises which includes the worldwide licensing of Elvis-related products and ventures including the 2022 film, Elvis. Her estate is reported to own Graceland, the home of Elvis Presley, as well as its contents which includes her father's personal effects. Of course, the IRS will be keen on what is reported as the value of her estate. The IRS may conduct its own valuation and may challenge her estate's valuation as they have with Michael Jackson's, Prince's, and Elvis'.

# Avoiding Probate – Funding a Revocable Trust

Now let's move onto how to fund a Revocable Trust. There are 2 ways. On the one hand, for real estate and certain personal property, we re-title them specifically into the Trust. For example, we re-title the family home into the Trust. If you have a mortgage, get approval from the mortgage company before making any transfer. If the spouses do not have more than a combined $27,220,000 in 2024 or have any reason to keep their property separate, then a joint Revocable Trust is in order. In Illinois, the State gives us one nice asset protection tool for the family home. It now allows us to hold the home as TBE (creditors cannot attach unless they have a judgment against both spouses) as well as in the name of your Revocable Trust. So, it allows us to avoid probate while giving us asset protection, which is a sweet deal.

For rental property, the first step would be to move it into a separate vehicle like a Limited Liability Company (LLC) and have the LLC owners be the Revocable Trust. If there is a lawsuit brought because of the rental property, any damage from this lawsuit should be limited to the property inside the LLC and leaves unexposed the assets outside of the LLC. But you must keep assets separate from the LLC and not commingle (share) personal and business assets, or you may defeat the asset protection of the LLC.

Lastly, we move bank accounts into the Revocable Trust. Or at least we try. Since the financial meltdown around 2008, banks have enacted more rules about re-titling real estate and bank accounts. Some banks tell my clients that they have to close their personal accounts and open up Trust accounts. The banks seem to think we are trying to set up irrevocable trusts that give asset protection. This is not what we are trying to achieve. We are trying to move the bank accounts into the names of revocable trusts to avoid probate. Revocable Trusts do not offer any creditor protection to the Grantors who set up the Trusts during their lifetimes. The bank accounts are still reported under the person's social security number. An alternative to re-titling is to have the banks make the accounts Pay on Death (POD) to the Revocable Trust.

On the other hand, for certain personal property, we do not re-title them into Revocable Trusts but instead change the beneficiaries. These include the beneficiaries under life insurance and retirement accounts (e.g., IRA's and 401K's). We do not re-title retirement accounts into the Revocable Trusts because the IRS may see it as you totally withdrawing all the funds and present you with a tax bill. So, again, we do not re-title these assets; we change the beneficiaries. The SECURE Act of 2020 changed the distribution rules for inherited IRA's, among other things. SECURE 2.0 was signed into law on December 29, 2022 and brought sweeping changes for retirement plans. Because of the tax implications, it is recommended that you speak with your investment advisor about maximizing the planning opportunities when designating beneficiaries for your IRA's and 401K's.

Effective January 1, 2020, Illinois enacted a new trust code. Previously, if somebody were a beneficiary under a trust, they would be notified by simply receiving a copy of the specific provision naming them as beneficiary and telling them what they got. Effective with the new legislation, they may be entitled to get a complete copy of the trust upon request.

# Pour-over Will

So far we have discussed how it is important to have a Revocable Trust in place and have certain assets re-titled into it or beneficiaries designated to it during your lifetime to avoid probate. Another key document is the Pour-over Will. A client of mine explained it this way: I am poor. It's over. Leave me alone. However, that is not the point of the Pour-over Will. It is to get anything that was not re-titled or did not have a change of beneficiary designation made prior to your death into your Revocable Trust. This means that if it is over $100,000 in personal property or any real estate, it will have to be probated, but it will pour-over into your Revocable Trust (which by virtue of your death becomes irrevocable).

My client who offered the explanation of the Pour-over Will also is the father of 3 grown daughters. I have 2 sons so I feel our family lives are quite different although children in general, like their parents, can be demanding. When he passes away, he wants to have an open casket in which he is holding a check. He knows his wife will stand back, and his 3 daughters will fight for it. However, he will have the last laugh … the check will bounce.

# Powers of Attorneys

As noted, there are 2 durable Powers of Attorney – one for medical decisions and one for financial decisions. In Illinois, our State legislature wants everyone to appoint one agent at a time to avoid ugly fights. Also, they made a point to note that although your agent is referred to as your attorney-in-fact, that does not make them attorneys. They still must go to law school for that. They are simply your agents but have fiduciary duties (legal responsibilities) to take care of you when they are acting under the Powers of Attorney (POA's).

A client of mine called and told me that his mother had passed away. He had her durable Power of Attorney for Property and was going to use it. I told him that they are not that durable. They are called durable because they remain effective after you become incompetent but not beyond your death.

The Power of Attorney for Healthcare allows your agent to speak for you when you cannot make medical decisions for yourself including the release of medical records under HIPAA, and life support and organ donation decisions. The point is for your agent to agree ahead of time to act as your agent and for him/her to know  what your wishes are for medical decisions. The form tries to make it easier on all those involved at a difficult time in your life (when you cannot speak for yourself). So, the medical form has you choose who will make those medical decisions – your agent, your physician, or never to pull the plug. Also, it gives you the option to decide between quality or quantity of life when the end is near.

For many years, Casey Kasem was the voice of America's Top 40 radio show and the voice behind many famous cartoons including Shaggy in the Scooby-Doo cartoons. Casey was worth an allegedly $80 million upon his death, but the dispute was not over his wealth but his care in his final days. He was married to his 2nd wife for over 30 years. In his final days, after a bitter fight, his daughter from his 1st marriage was named temporary conservator over the objections of his 2nd wife. In direct defiance of the court's order, his 2nd wife removed him from his nursing home in the dead of the night. By the time he was located, his condition had significantly deteriorated and soon after he passed. However, that was not the end of the fight. His children argued that their father wanted to be buried in the U.S. His 2nd wife took his body and had him cremated in Oslo, Norway. Some had speculated that the body was removed from the U.S. to prevent a possible elder abuse investigation.

*Casey Kasem*

Remember, powers of attorneys are durable because they remain effective even if you become incompetent. So, if you appoint trusted family or friends to make financial or medical decisions, they can speak for you when you cannot.

In early 2022, the family of actor, Bruce Willis, announced that he had aphasia, a condition that affects a person's ability to speak or comprehend language. In early 2023, his family announced that Bruce had been diagnosed with frontotemporal dementia (FTD). This is a private family

*Bruce Willis*

matter involving very difficult life changes. Those with FTD may exhibit inappropriate social behavior; lack empathy, judgment or inhibition; or repetitive, compulsive behavior. Sadly, these conditions only get progressively worse. Bruce's extended family from his two marriages have stoically aided him during this devastating time. Because there has not been any news of a guardianship proceeding needed for Bruce, it would seem that he had POAs, which would remain valid beyond his incapacity.

If a loved one is exhibiting startling changes in behavior, a neuropsychological evaluation may provide critical insight as to why and establish a crucial baseline to monitor if such behavior worsens, so steps can be taken to protect the loved ones such as utilizing the POAs or seeking to establish a guardianship for their care.

*President Jimmy Carter*

In February, 2023, the family of Jimmy Carter, the 39th President of the United States, announced that he was in hospice at his family home in Plains, GA, instead of staying in a hospital for his remaining time. End-of-life care is best coordinated with the person's POA, their attending physician and hospice care workers. The goal of having a POA is to lay out your wishes, reducing the stress (and possible guilt) of decision-making to be made by family members. It is important to talk with those you wish to appoint and make sure they are comfortable with the responsibility, and, if so, for them to know specifically what your wishes are.

The Power of Attorney for Property allows your agent to speak for you when you cannot and make financial decisions for you including filing tax returns and access to bank accounts. Remember to coordinate the appointment of the successor Trustee in your Revocable Trust with your appointment of agent in the Power of Attorney for Property.

# Guardianship Proceedings

Having Powers of Attorney for Healthcare and Property in place will help avoid the need for guardianship proceedings. Probate proceedings are for deceased's estates and for disabled individuals. In a probate proceeding for a disabled individual, an agent is appointed as a guardian of the estate (finances)  and guardian of the person (health). One person may serve in both capacities. A guardianship proceeding is a legal proceeding almost always open to the public. It is the adjudication of the person's disability. Once a guardian is appointed, there is court supervision (regular accounting before the court) until that person's death or recovery from incompetency. It could be very costly. The estate of the alleged disabled person may have to pay for up to 3 sets of attorneys – the attorneys arguing for both sides of the disabled person and the guardian ad litem, an attorney appointed by the court to independently supervise the disabled individual.

Most court battles like this can be avoided if the proper durable Powers of Attorney are in place prior to being needed. In all my years of practicing law, I have consistently found that my clients are driven by a strong motivator: the desire to remain in control. Do proper planning now, and achieve that result!

Brian Wilson of The Beach Boys is a heartbreaking genius in the music industry. As the band's lead songwriter, he was responsible for the Beach Boys' iconic sound. But, as the weight of fame took its toll, he retreated behind the scenes to continue his music-making passion. He also took psychedelic drugs that damaged his mental faculties. Further, at these

*Brian Wilson*

troubling crossroads, a Rasputin-type individual gained control of Brian's life. But luckily for Brian, he had a friend, Melinda, who would be pivotal in launching the court battle that would remove this Rasputin from Brian's life but only after this individual had Brian rewrite his Will and provide 70% to go to him. Fortunately, the court later nullified that Will citing undue influence. Brian married Melinda and appointed her power of attorney of his healthcare decisions, but he did not name a successor. His money is held in trust and managed by long-time business confidants. Sadly, Brian has been suffering from dementia, and since Melinda passed away after 28 years of marriage in January, 2024, he has been in a severe mental tailspin. Because there was no successor named in his Healthcare Power of Attorney, his long-time business confidants had to go to court to be appointed Brian's guardian of the person, that is, responsible for his medical decisions. Their goal is to safeguard Brian from himself and others, while allowing him to live his fullest life possible with these safeguards in place. Naming agents to serve if you are not competent is very challenging, but typically it is better for you to make that decision instead of leaving it up to the courts.

In 2011, Steven Tyler, the lead singer of Aerosmith, wrote his memoir, *"Does the Noise in My Head Bother You?"* in which he detailed his sexual exploits of a teenager, who had come from a very troubled family life. He persuaded her mother, who had mental health issues, to let him have guardianship over the teenager. He told the mother it was to allow him to put her daughter in better schools but, as he put it in the book, it was so he wouldn't get arrested if he took her out of state. He never enrolled her in school but took her on the road touring.

In 2019, California waived for three years the statute of limitations for childhood sexual abuse. Days before it ended, Julia Holcomb Misley, filed a lawsuit accusing Mr. Tyler of intentionally inflicting emotional distress, sexual battery, and sexual assault of a minor. Ms. Misley claims she had just turned 16 when she met Mr. Tyler in 1973 after a concert in Portland, and for three years thereafter it was sex, drugs and a forced abortion. A 1997 Aerosmith autobiography also graphically detailed the exploitation. With so much evidence supplied by Mr. Tyler in the 1997 band autobiography and the 2011 personal memoir, Ms. Misley appears to have a strong case.

*Steven Tyler*

What heightened this depravity was that Mr. Tyler knew that he had to have some sort of legal papers to protect himself from charges of sex-trafficking of a minor if he crossed state lines. Having read what is publicly available to date – the Complaint and Answer – although it is called a guardianship, probably it is Powers of Attorney that were signed. They give similar powers but no safeguards and protections that are part of the court guardianship process. There is no judge who could examine the proposed guardian-disabled relationship. No Guardian Ad Litem possibly appointed as an independent third party to check in on the disabled individual and confirm that the relationship is in her best interests.

In Mr. Tyler's Answer, he raises affirmative defenses that he believes gives reason for why he cannot be liable for sexual exploitation of Ms. Misley when she was a minor because Ms. Misley's claims "are barred in whole or in part because of immunity or qualified immunity to [Mr. Tyler] as caregiver and/or guardian." To me, this is a bombshell because he admits that he was Ms. Misley's caregiver and/or guardian which means he had a legal duty as a fiduciary to take care of Ms. Misley. Presumably sexually exploiting her as a minor would breach his legal duty of care. Mr. Tyler also states as an affirmative defense that Ms. Misley's claims "are barred in whole or in part by Ms. Misley's consent." Someone who has a guardian is incapable of giving consent. Mr. Tyler has also raised as an affirmative defense that Mr. Tyler's "alleged conduct is protected under the First Amendment of the United States Constitution," which states: "Congress shall make no law respecting an establishment of religion or prohibiting the free exercise thereof; or abridging the freedom of speech, or of the press; or the right of the people peaceably to assemble, and to petition the Government for a redress of grievances." Presumably Mr. Tyler is stating that he exercised his First Amendment right of free speech when he wrote his memoir and the band did its autobiography. Yes; he has the right to say it. And Ms. Misley can use what Mr. Tyler said against him.

But there are so many questions. How many times did Mr. Tyler use this legal mechanism to cross state lines with a minor he was having sex with under the guise of being that minor's legal agent? Who told him of this shameful ruse?

This is not a story of simply someone who went to a concert and became a groupie, having sex with the band. This was premeditated sexual exploitation of a minor, and from how Mr. Tyler put it, sadly he had his act down pat.

Next is an example of what happens when the court has to step in because you do not have Powers of Attorney in place. Who remembers the Marx Brothers' movies, Duck Soup, Animal Crackers and more?

The Marx Brothers made over 2 dozen comedies. Half of them Groucho made with his brothers Chico and Harpo. In his time, Groucho Marx was a wildly successful comedian and film and television star. He had quick wit, and, for audiences in the 1930's-1950's, his comedy act was the definition of politically incorrect. In his late career, Groucho starred in You Bet your Life where when the guest said the secret word, the duck with a cigar dropped down.

When he was about 84 years old, Groucho's son thought he was not acting with a full deck. He took Groucho to court to be appointed his guardian. But Groucho's 36-year-old girlfriend, Ms. Fleming, thought she had his best interests at heart. Unfortunately all of this had to play out in probate court. The judge actually ended up appointing Groucho's grandson as his guardian.

*Groucho Marx*

In February, 2024, the very troubling documentary "Where is Wendy Williams?" premiered on Lifetime. This follows Ms. Williams openly discussing on her past long-running talk show, "The Wendy Williams Show," her cocaine and alcohol addictions, her stays in sober houses, and her medical diagnosis of Graves' disease and lymphedema.

*Wendy Williams*

Towards the end of her show's run, she exhibited dangerous behavior including fainting on live TV. Following her bank, Wells Fargo, freezing her accounts and seeking a guardianship (known as a conservatorship in New York), attorney Sabrina Morrissey was appointed Ms. Williams' guardian.

In the Vulture magazine interview, "Wendy Williams Documentary [Executive Producers] Say They Had Her Best Interests At Heart," one of the Executive Producers, Mark Ford, said the contract for the Lifetime documentary was entered under the guardianship and everything shot was under the guardianship. That means Ms. Morrissey, as guardian, signed the contract for the Lifetime documentary on her ward, Ms. Williams. Ms. Morrissey appears to have broad powers over Ms. Williams including what she is allowed to do (drink heavily with the cameras rolling) and not to do (see her family).

Wendy Williams, herself, is listed as an Executive Producer! It seems implausible that a ward of the court in Ms. Williams' state could have the mental faculties to be an Executive Producer. Right before the launch of the premiere, in addition to all the other ailments Ms. Williams is suffering from, it was announced that she had been diagnosed with frontotemporal dementia and aphasia. Apparently the diagnosis was made public in April, 2023, coincidentally just when the filming wrapped.

Although Ms. Morrissey signed the contract for the documentary, the weekend before its premiere she went to court seeking to prevent its release with a temporary restraining order. The judge tossed it out on the grounds that it would violate Ms. Willams' First Amendment right to free speech. But obviously Ms. Williams is in no state to speak for herself. The documentary seems entirely exploitative. As Ms. Williams' guardian, when the screen credits roll and show Ms. Williams' name as one of the Executive Producers, it is legally the same as showing Ms. Morrissey's name. So how bizarre for Ms. Morrissey to sue to stop the airing of the documentary when she signed off on it.

And the behavior, not the least of which is Ms. Williams' enormous drinking in the documentary, just questions whether Ms. Morrisey is doing her job of protecting Ms. Williams or exploiting her. Mr. Ford, one of the Executive Producers, stated they stopped filming the documentary when it became apparent that there was something wrong with Ms. Williams. With how severely impaired Ms. Williams looks while they were shooting, it begs the question: Why not shelve the project? Ms. Williams is under a guardianship with severe mental and physical disabilities. Ms. Morrissey sounds like Jaime Spears, Britney Spears' father, who was her guardian and made her work during the entire guardianship, which in hindsight looks wildly exploitative because Mr. Spears' salary allegedly included a percentage of what Britney earned.

A big problem is that Ms. Williams' case is under seal, so the public does not know how Ms. Williams is doing and what exactly Ms. Morrissey, as her guardian, is doing to help her. In my opinion, the silver lining in this documentary is that it showed the guardrails are off, and sadly no one is looking out for Ms. Williams, not even her court-appointed guardian, Ms. Morrissey.

When you hear "Britney Spears," what do you think? Mouseketeer? Singer, dancer, performer? Celebrity who had one of the most public nervous breakdowns? Or, perhaps her decade-plus guardianship?

Britney had not had any control over her personal and financial decisions following her breakdown almost a decade and a half

*Britney Spears*

ago. Her father was part of a team court-appointed as her guardian of her person (healthcare) and of her estate (finances). The team was appointed as plenary guardian (unlimited). A guardian is appointed by the court when it is determined that someone cannot possibly take care of themselves. It is not a decision taken lightly.

Be aware that competency is a fluid thing. Someone may be incompetent at a certain time and competent another. If competent for a lasting time, a guardian isn't needed.

Not the only strange item in this case was that Britney's father, Jamie Spears, as her guardian, appeared to be compensated for his role for caring for his daughter's finances with what seemed to be a base salary of $16,000/monthly but also a percentage of her income generated. Now we were not talking about him managing her stock portfolio but her performing. Supposedly she earned well over $100 million for her 4-year Vegas residency alone. If, for example, her dad, as her guardian, is paid 1 1/2% (as it is reported), her dad would have received $1,500,000. If Britney was able to perform so successfully, it begged the question if she was competent. Lastly, her father's compensation arrangement sounded like a serious conflict of interest. What was he looking out for: his daughter's financial well-being or his paycheck? Note because a guardian had been appointed, Britney paid not only for her attorney fees, but the other parties' attorney's fees as well!

While Britney's breakdown played out in public, her hopeful recovery for the most part had occurred behind closed doors. Well, those doors were blown wide-open when she spoke on her own behalf on a conference call with the court for her guardianship update. It was via phone, rather than in person in court, due to the pandemic. However, this also was a benefit to her because she is unrelentingly hounded by the paparazzi. Variety included a "lightly edited transcript." Britney exposed incredible details about her dubious care, the inexplicable demands placed on her by the conservatorship, and her impassioned desired – to be in control of her body, money, career and life. If bad things have been happening to her, things had to change. Guardianships are to protect the incompetent individual, not abuse them. They are public proceedings for that very reason.

Bessemer Trust resigned as co-conservator of Britney's estate (finances) the day after its appointment, citing Britney's impassioned court testimony and her request to terminate the "voluntary" conservatorship. This was explosive because it implied that, for all these years, she could end the conservatorship at any time. However, in her testimony, Britney stated point-blank that no one told her she could petition the court to terminate her conservatorship. Most is unknown about the conservatorship because it has been sealed, kept out of the public eye, which is unusual and runs counter to their goal of keeping it public for the individual's best interests. Following her testimony, even more startling, her "voluntary" conservatorship came to an abrupt end.

However, things have been grim basically since the termination of her guardianship. Because she is a mega-celebrity, every public move is scrutinized. Her posts on social media and her public outings have only gotten more bizarre and worrisome. At times you would think someone would have the sense to turn off her social media pages, but, with how she has been acting, it is probably for the better that they have stayed on.

# Appointment of Agent for Disposition of Remains

Lastly, for a good estate plan, you should have an Appointment of Agent for Disposition of Remains whereby your agent is able to dispose of your body after you have passed. You can specifically state where you want to be buried or if you want to be cremated. You also can give your agent the discretion to overrule your cremation wishes. For the most part, if it is legal, you can put it in your estate plan.

*Hunter Thompson*

Hunter Thompson was a gonzo journalist who lived larger than life. Some of his books were turned into movies like *Fear and Loathing in Vegas* which starred Johnny Depp. Apparently Hunter and Johnny were good friends. Hunter allegedly killed himself when he was terminally ill. Hunter had let it be known that following his death, he wanted to be cremated and have his ashes shot out of a cannon by Johnny Depp. And, he was.

Even if you do not want to end it with a BOOM! like Hunter, there are many options for what to do after you pass including burial, cremation, or human composting. With 8,000,000,000 inhabitants on Earth, space is running short on a lot of things including burial. Some opt for cremation and direct their loved ones where to scatter their ashes. Human composting is gaining popularity because it is not as harsh on the planet. Burial requires space whereas cremation the burning of fossil fuels. Remember, laying out your wishes now should make a difficult time less stressful after your passing.

# Estate & Gift Taxes

Now, let's shift gears. Let's talk about federal and Illinois estate and gift taxes. Why? Because you never know when you might need it.

First, let's talk about federal estate and gift taxes. Federal gift taxes were enacted in 1924. We have had federal estate taxes since 1916. The federal estate tax exemption amount increased from $30,000 in 1916 to $1,000,000 in 2009. It was briefly done away with in 2010. I thought billionaires in hospitals would be very nervous, but no "accidents" were reported. In 2011, the federal estate tax exemption amount came back and at a happily raised rate of $5,000,000 per individual. It is indexed with inflation which means it automatically increases every year. In 2024, the unified federal estate and gift tax exemption amount is $13,610,000 so a married couple can gift during their lifetime or at their deaths a combined $27,220,000.

In 2024, you can also gift $18,000 annually to anyone. If it is cash, the IRS isn't interested. It is worthwhile to note that there is no annual limit on cash gifts made directly for tuition or medical expenses. If it is non-cash, the IRS will want a gift tax return (Form 709). You won't owe any taxes (unless all your taxable gifts exceed $13,610,000 in 2024) but the non-cash gifts or gifts of cash over $18,000 annually to each person are reported. The IRS likes to keep tabs on these reportable gifts. Again, you can gift during your lifetime or upon your death, $13,610,000 tax-free before the IRS will come looking for you. Anything over a net taxable estate of $13,610,000 is taxed at 40%.

It is important to note that gifts made within 3 years of death are counted as part of your estate, which may impact whether you have to pay federal estate taxes. Married couples have $27,220,000 in 2024 that they can give away during their lifetimes or following their deaths. If one does not use up his/her complete $13,610,000, the remaining portion of it is portable to the surviving spouse. A nifty concept if your estates are that big.

There are a few transfers that are exempt from federal gift and estate taxes. That is, you don't have to pay. First, transfers to spouses and charities are exempt from gift and estate taxes. Annual gifts of up to $18,000 in cash to anyone are exempt. Any payment made directly to a healthcare provider or education provider is exempt from the gift tax. Many clients take advantage of these tax breaks to pay for their grandchildren's tuition or other financial assistance.

If the law is not extended, as of January 1, 2026, the federal estate tax exemption will decrease to about $7,000,000 per individual (from $13,610,000 in 2024) and to about $14,000,000 per married couple (from $27,220,000 in 2024).

Now, let's talk about Illinois estate and gift taxes. Illinois lifetime estate tax exemption is $4,000,000. Any amounts over that and you will owe the State of Illinois estate taxes following your death, and that is on the very first dollar, not that over $4,000,000. Furthermore, the unused $4,000,000 is not portable to the surviving spouse. Note that in 2024 a bill has been proposed to increase the Illinois lifetime estate tax lifetime exemption to $6,000,000, but it has not been enacted into law. Unlike some other States, Illinois luckily does not have a gift tax.

# Advanced Estate Planning – Give up Control

With the looming January 1, 2026 deadline when the federal estate and gift tax exemption plummets, now is the time to explore the alphabet soup of advanced estate planning – SLATs, QPRTs, ILITs, DAPTs, CRTs and more.

For such an estate plan to be properly evaluated, it is necessary to have all of your advisors involved in the discussion. That includes your attorney, accountant, insurance agent, and investment advisor. Equally important in advanced estate planning is that you must evaluate how much money and which assets you require to maintain your lifestyle. These assets will not be a part of your advanced estate planning.

During 2024, the federal estate and gift tax exemption is $13,610,000 per individual and $27,220,000 per married couple with portability of one spouse's unused federal estate tax exemption going to the surviving spouse. The Illinois estate tax exemption is $4,000,000 per individual but does not have the portability of the unused state estate tax exemption for the surviving spouse to use. Also, if your estate exceeds $4,000,000, Illinois taxes your estate at about 16% starting on the very first $1, not that which is over its $4,000,000 exemption.

As you are aware, the current federal estate and gift tax exemption is set to drop to pre-2018 levels (adjusted for inflation) as of January 1, 2026, and is estimated to decrease to somewhere between $6,000,000-$7,000 000 per individual and $12,000,000-$14,000,000 per married couple. Also, it is important to note that estate planning is based on current tax law, which is subject to change from time to time and at any time. In other words, there is no guarantee as to what the tax rates will be in the future and which tax vehicles the IRS may challenge.

Here are some advanced estate planning options for your consideration:

1. A Spousal Lifetime Access Trust (SLAT) is an irrevocable trust whereby you could move assets tax-free up to the amount of the current federal estate exemption of $13,610,000. Please note that the IRS has stated that if the federal estate exemption falls as scheduled by 50% as of January 1, 2026, there will not be a clawback of the excess exemption utilized when it was available. A SLAT can be set up for each spouse but mindful of the Reciprocal Trust Doctrine. Also, we cannot have the spouses in essentially the same financial position they were in before the SLATs. The donor-spouse gets the indirect benefit of the assets from the beneficiary-spouse. Yet, we are careful to use a floating spouse definition in case of the untimely death or divorce of the beneficiary-spouse.

2. For a vacation home, you can transfer it into a Qualified Personal Residence Trust (QPRT), which is an irrevocable trust that removes the property from your estate. The trust is set up so that you would be able to take advantage of your vacation home for a certain number of years, say 10. After that, your children, or whomever you want, would own the home. Technically, you would be responsible for paying rent if you stayed there. However, there are options such as your children gifting you money so that your payment of rent would be a wash. If you died during the term of the trust, the vacation home would be included in your taxable estate. In other words, you would lose that amount of the federal exemption that you took advantage of.

3. A Spousal Lifetime Access Non-Grantor Trust or SLANT is similar to the SLAT, but it is a non-grantor trust, whereby the tax attributes would flow through to the beneficiaries of the trust, and not be reported on the grantor's tax return. Non-grantor trusts are particularly useful for asset protection.

4. A Domestic Asset Protection Trust or DAPT is a self-settled trust which must be established in one of the states that allows them. DAPTs are particularly important to individuals in professions exposed to heightened litigation such as doctors, dentists, and lawyers.

5. A Grantor Retained Trust is a tax planning vehicle which is especially attractive when interest rates are low. However, we currently are in a high inflationary period which presumably will last through the scheduled sunset of the federal estate and gift tax exemption.

6. Another estate planning option is to make contributions either now such as in a charitable lead trust or at a later time such as in a charitable remainder trust. These too are irrevocable trusts. These are important tax planning vehicles for those charitably-inclined.

7. An Irrevocable Life Insurance Trust (ILIT) owns life insurance on your life and is excluded from your taxable estate. If you originally own life insurance in your name and move it into an ILIT, then there is a 3-year window that must pass for it to be excluded from your estate.

Time is running out to structure, implement and fund advanced estate planning vehicles at the currently high exemption levels. Your options should involve a comprehensive discussion with all of your trusted advisors, so you are able to make your decision as to which direction you would like to take to minimize your estate and gift taxes, maximize asset protection, and provide to the greatest extent for your loved ones.

# Advanced Estate Planning – Keep Control

Now let's talk about advanced estate planning whereby you retain control. Remember, advanced estate planning is needed where your estate is too big. How big is too big? Usually clients want to do advanced estate planning if their estate exceeds the federal estate tax exemption which is $13,610,000 per person in 2024.  That means that married couples can take advantage of passing $27,220,000 worth of assets tax-free to their children, grandchildren, and other beneficiaries. So if they are above that number, we talk. Here's what we talk about.

First is a limited partnership with a corporate general partner. I know. Sexy, right? Clients move assets that they do not live off of – major investment accounts, vacation homes, etc. Again, assets that they do not need for everyday living expenses. Once in the limited partnership, it is still in the client's estate. However, they then gift portions of the limited partnership to their children. Specifically they are gifting limited partner interests to the children. A general partner interest allows someone to run the show. A limited partner interest allows them to sit on the sidelines and watch what is going on but have no voice or control in the management of the partnership. This allows the parents to maintain control while at the same time finding out if the children really want to become involved in the family business. Any interests owned by the children reduce the parents' estates and IRS tax bill.

Note above that there is a corporate general partner. Remember, the general partner runs the show and takes the risks. A corporation helps limit the liability to what is in it. So, when we have a limited partnership run by a corporate general partner, there is basically nothing in the corporation. Nothing really is legally required to be in it. If we could not structure it this way, most people would not be willing to run anything, knowing that everything they owned was at risk. No one could sleep at night. The law balances this with the concept of fiduciary duty, which is the duty the owners, directors and officers owe to a corporation including for loyalty and care.

Second is a limited liability company with voting and nonvoting shares and series. There is a lot going on here, but the main point is for the owners to retain control. A limited liability company if treated properly does just that – limits the liability of the owner. That means keep business separate from pleasure and jump through all the federal and state hoops (including open business bank account, and file annual state report and federal and state tax returns). It gives you protection from creditors. Again, the goal here is to gift to the clients' children nonvoting interests. Let them get their feet wet in the family business and see if they are interested in one day taking it over. By gifting nonvoting interests, the parents remain in control, but the value of their estate is decreased by the gifts to the children. Setting up series means basically setting up divisions which means segregating liability. If something unfortunate happens in one series, it does not jeopardize the entire business venture.

I've been told you can get married at least 3 times - for love, for money and for the Hell of it. Not necessarily in that order. There was a client who reminisced about his "I do's" turning into "I don't". His father owns a lot of real estate along the Gold Coast in Chicago. The name of the neighborhood says it all. He was happy when his son got engaged. However, he wanted his son to be married for himself, not what he was in line to inherit. Over 6 months before the wedding, he pulled his son aside and told him that he wouldn't inherit anything unless his bride signed a prenuptial agreement which says what yours is yours and what's mine is mine. The son knew his bride was marrying for love and so had no problem asking her to sign a prenuptial agreement. However, she wouldn't give him an answer. He asked her again several times and then the night before the wedding. Finally she told him that she wasn't going to sign the prenuptial agreement, knowing that guests had flown in from across the U.S. for the wedding. That night, the bride flew home. The next day the groom and his family threw a big party with the groom surrounded by single ladies and being the most eligible bachelor at the bar. The takeaway here is that a prenuptial agreement keeps property separate before marriage, separate after. This does not take the romance out of marriage, but the 60% divorce rate probably does.

# Nothing is Certain Except Death & Taxes

For a number of years, there has been talk about raising the capital gains tax rates to equal the individual income tax rates. Currently the maximum long-term capital gains tax rate is about 50% less than the top individual tax rate. So some individuals with very valuable assets have been selling them. And there is no better example of this being done then by artists with valuable music catalogs.

To kick off 2023, Justin Bieber sold his music catalog for a reported $200 million.

Previously Bob Dylan sold his for a reported $300-$400 million. Neil Young sold 50% of his catalog for an estimated $150 million. Imagine Dragons sold their current complete catalog for about $100 million. A bunch more have sold their catalogs for an undisclosed price including Katy Perry, the Estate of Whitney Houston, David Crosby, Barry Manilow, Blondie, Chrissy Hynes' interest in her band The Pretenders, Tina Turner, Shakira, and, last but not least, Lindsey Buckingham, Stevie Nicks, Christine McVie and Mick Fleetwood of Fleetwood Mac.

*Justin Bieber*

One artist who bucked the trend of selling their music catalogs is Taylor Swift, whose current goal is to retain control and ownership of her music catalog. At 34, she is worth a reported $1.1 billion, due in large part to her incredibly successful Eras tour.

*Taylor Swift*

Her first six albums (Taylor Swift, Fearless, Speak Now, Red, 1989 and Reputation) were done when she was with Big Machine Records (BMR). During this collaboration, BMR and Taylor signed off on licensing for her songs from these albums to be in such things as commercials. In 2018, Taylor moved to Republic Records, which is owned by Universal Music Group. In 2019, Scooter Braun's Ithaca Holdings bought BMR. Taylor wants to have nothing to do with Scooter and has refused to permit the licensing of any of her songs from the initial master recordings of these first six albums. She took a decisive step in 2019 when she announced she was going to re-record her first six albums. And she has done so and released these new recordings of her first six albums as Taylor's Versions. Now she owns the master recordings where she can license these songs however she sees fit, and she gets a larger royalty percentage. In addition to being a fabulous songwriter, singer, musician, and performer, Taylor is a phenomenal businesswoman.

## Simply the Best

*Tina Turner*

It is only fitting for us to pay homage to the one…the only…the unmistakable Tina Turner. Much-beloved Tina Turner passed away in May 2023 at the age of 83. Immediately in her honor Australians rejoicing in her image and energy tried to set a new record line-dancing to her critically-acclaimed homespun *"Nutbush City Limits"*. It is a semi-autobiographical song written by Tina commemorating her hometown. Although Tennessee was fortunate to be Tina's birthplace, she was fond of Switzerland where her husband and biggest fan, Erwin Bach, was, and of Europe where her massive fanbase was (dwarfing the U.S.). Her two biological sons (Craig and Ronnie) sadly preceded her in death, leaving behind two surviving adopted sons (Ike, Jr. and Michael). Her estate of about $250 million will pass under Swiss law, Tina having renounced her U.S. citizenship a few years before her death. Her high octane performances and passionate talent made her a driving force in music, film, style and living life to its fullest.

# Final Words – There Are No Heirs Until You Pass

The concept of Nepo Babies has come up again in the entertainment news. It refers to nepotism and for those celebrities who use their fame to launch the careers of their children. You may think of Drew Barrymore who comes from a long lineage of Hollywood greats, including Ethyl, Lionel, and John Barrymore. The singer Elle King is Rob Schneider's daughter. Jennifer Aniston is John Aniston's daughter. The actor George Clooney's aunt was the actress and singer Rosemary Clooney. Kiefer Sutherland is Donald Sutherland's son. Peter Fonda is Henry Fonda's son. Jane Fonda is Henry's daughter. Ben Stiller was Jerry Stiller's son. Josh Brolin is James Brolin's son. Charlie Sheen and Emilio Estevez are Martin Sheen's sons. Rob Reiner is Carl Reiner's son. Michael Douglas is Kirk Douglas' son. Angelica Huston is John Huston's daughter. But this goes back far, presumably since the founding of Hollywood.

A number of celebrities have come out and declared that when they pass, their children will not get their inheritance.

Marie Osmond has stated, "I don't know anybody who becomes anything if they're just handed money."

*Marie Osmond*

# CELEBRITIES' LESSONS IN ESTATE PLANNING | 57

Guy Fieri of "Diners, Drive-In's and Dives", has been a long-time fixture on the Food Network. Recently he cemented a three-year $100 million deal. He's become outspoken saying that his children will not receive anything when he passes unless they get two degrees, meaning both undergraduate and postgraduate. So kids, listen up! Your parent cannot disinherit their spouse, but they can disinherit their children as we learned in the case of Aaron Spelling, the late great TV mogul.

*Guy Fieri*

Warren Buffett recommended, "Leave the children enough so that they can do anything but not enough that they can do nothing."

*Warren Buffett*

Sting has said, "What comes in we spend, and there isn't much left. I certainly don't want to leave them trust funds that are albatrosses around their necks. They have to work."

Daniel Craig, probably best known as James Bond, said "My philosophy is to get rid of it, or give it away before you go."

*Sting*

Gordon Ramsay of Hell's Kitchen believes to avoid spoiling his children, he has no intention of leaving his money to them when he dies.

Although all of this may seem harsh, celebrities oftentimes assist their children

*Daniel Craig*

in ways that others cannot. They help them get into industries and careers where many cannot unless you know someone. Having that leg up is invaluable.

Also, I hope I live long enough to see celebrities truly give their money away. Have Bill Gates and Warren Buffett give their money to foundations that are not run by people of their choosing where it looks like they have remained in control.

*Gordon Ramsay*

Disclaimer: This is not intended as legal advice. Consult with an attorney for professional advice.

**Photo Credits**

| | |
|---|---|
| DMX: | hurricanehank / Shutterstock.com |
| Chadwick Boseman: | DFree / Shutterstock.com |
| Herman Cain: | Kathy Hutchins / Shutterstock.com |
| Prince: | Northfoto / Shutterstock.com |
| Anthony Chia-Hua Hsieh: | ZUMA Press, Inc. / Alamy Stock Photo |
| Tom Benson: | UPI / Alamy Stock Photo |
| Gina Lollobrigida: | Denis Makarenko / Shutterstock.com |
| Aretha Franklin: | Pictorial Press Ltd / Alamy Stock Photo |
| Heath Ledger: | carrie-nelson / Shutterstock.com |
| Larry King: | Featureflash Photo Agency / Shutterstock.com |
| Tom Clancy: | Richard Ellis / Alamy Stock Photo |
| David Bowie: | JStone / Shutterstock.com |
| Michael Jackson: | landmarkmedia / Shutterstock.com |
| Bing Crosby: | MARKA / Alamy Stock Photo |
| Whitney Houston: | Helga Esteb / Shutterstock.com |
| Aaron Spelling: | Featureflash Photo Agency / Shutterstock.com |
| Lisa Marie Presley: | Tinseltown / Shutterstock.com |
| Casey Kasem: | s_bukley / Shutterstock.com |
| Bruce Willis: | Featureflash Photo Agency / Shutterstock.com |
| Jimmy Carter: | GL Archive / Alamy Stock Photo |
| Brian Wilson: | s_bukley / Shutterstock.com |
| Steven Tyler: | The Photo Access / Alamy Stock Photo |
| Groucho Marx: | Mary Evans Picture Library / Alamy Stock Photo |
| Wendy Williams: | Kathy Hutchins / Shutterstock.com |
| Brittany Spears: | UPI / Alamy Stock Photo |
| Hunter Thompson: | Everett Collection Historical / Alamy Stock Photo |
| Justin Bieber: | Doug Peters / Alamy Stock Photo |
| Tina Turner: | MediaPunch Inc / Alamy Stock Photo |
| Taylor Swift: | Tinseltown / Shutterstock.com |
| Marie Osmond: | CarlaVanWagoner / Shutterstock.com |
| Guy Fieri: | Sipa USA / Alamy Stock Photo |
| Warren Buffett: | Geisler-Fotopress GmbH / Alamy Stock Photo |
| Sting: | Tinseltown / Shutterstock.com |
| Daniel Craig: | Featureflash Photo Agency / Shutterstock.com |
| Gordon Ramsay: | Featureflash Photo Agency / Shutterstock.com |

Made in the USA
Monee, IL
16 May 2024